Champagne Regained

Jacqueline Widmar Stewart
Champagne Regained

Edition Axel Menges

© 2013 Edition Axel Menges, Stuttgart / London
ISBN 978-3-936681-62-8
All rights reserved, including those of translation into other languages.

Printing and binding: Graspo CZ, a.s., Zlín, Czech Republic

Editing: Dorothea Duwe, Nora Krehl-von Mühlendahl
Design: Axel Menges

7	Foreword
8	The history
13	Champagne's illustrious widows
17	The process of champagne making
18	The land
19	The parks
21	References
22	Pictorial section
	Roman roots 22 – The Loire connection 30 – Troyes 34 – Bar-sur-Aube 40 – Provins 42 – Châlons-en-Champagne 48 – Lagny-sur-Marne 49 – Clicquot 50 – Pommery 52 – The craft of winemaking 60 – Montagne de Reims 72 – Cote des Blancs 78 – Cote de Sézanne 80 – Vallée de Marne 84 – Aube 88 – Terroir and chalky cliffs 92 – The cultural commerce centers of Reims and Epernay 96 – Le Parc naturel régional de la Montagne de Reims 112 – Le Parc naturel régional de la Forêt d'Orient 116

Foreword

An effervescent renaissance of a grand era

A certain eeriness haunts the narrow streets of Troyes, like the feeling that might have gripped the sea farers returning to Roanoke Island, or might have overtaken Evangeline's fellow villagers – a sense that some sudden turn of fate snatched stunning success from its longtime domain.

The rhythmical design of Troyes' timbered façades carry memories of a richly woven past. Along the canals the wind still carries the soft splashing sounds of barges laden with fine woolens, silks and cottons, bringing their wares into the houses that awaited their arrival.

Bonds had formed early at the edge of the forests, connecting Celts to Cistercians to Templars, forged in conical kilns where wood carbonized to charcoal.

Guilds passed down their symbols and kinship from age to age.

In the Comté of Champagne a dynamic scene once revolved around trading in a vast array of textile crafts by a cadre of European merchants.

Trade fairs already had started in Champagne in the 5th century, according to one source. At the edge of the Holy Roman Empire there grew a thriving and vibrant realm, a cloth-lovers' paradise devoted to sensuous textiles, fabrics and trade. One continuous annual trade fair divided among four cities, with two rounds each in its primary center of Troyes and Provins and one each in Bar-sur-Aube and Lagny, drew in Europeans and their wares.

Silk, woolens, linens, cottons abounded: linens from Provins, Reims, Troyes, Chalons, Lagny; muslin from Reims; cotton-linen fustian from Bar-sur-Aube.

For more than a century Champagne excelled as a center of international trade and finance.

In the early Middle Ages the counts of Champagne encouraged establishment of new villages and supported the arts. In the 12th century Chrétien de Troyes shone as a leading light of medieval literature, revered especially for his work on Arthurian subjects.

At the peak of its success, the fine-tuned scene featured canals that floated wares into the heart of town while keeping trout, carp and salmon at the ready for sumptuous meals.

13 hospitals provided health care; financiers transacted a bounty of business; the marc de Troyes gauge added precision to weights and measures.

Merchants gathered from all over the known world, trading, bartering, lending, shipping – time after time returning to the residences that waited for them and their wares. Under the auspices of local counts in the Comté of Champagne tradespeople formed a close-knit comity.

From all appearances that might be imagined a millennium later, the setting seemed roundly ecumenical. The work by St. Bernard of Clairvaux, early Cistercian reformer and community activist, strengthened Champagne's cohesiveness. The library of Troyes that was founded in the 12th century and expanded by the collection from Clairvaux remains a crown jewel in France today. Financings, barters, loans, banking and minting attracted high sophistication into the equation – the Lombards, and those from Cahors. Under the banner of the Holy Roman Empire increasing numbers of Galls, Romans, Franks, Spaniards, Italians, English, Dutch, Flemish, Germans gathered to exchange their dry goods, leathers, spices and precious woods and metals.

A sense of permanence and belonging flourished in neighborhoods: Rue de Montpellier, Hôtel des Allemands, Hôtel des Maures, Rue des Anciennes Tanneries, Rue de la Pierre, Rue Champeaux, Rue de la Montée des Changes, Place du Marché au Pain.

Then abruptly the scene changed from idyllic to empty, bustling to silent, ebullient to eerie.

The year 1285 destroyed Champagne, shattering its fortunes

Within a year following Philippe le Bel's marriage to Jeanne de Navarre, Champagne fell into a centuries-long slump. One hundred thousand Jews were banished from the region, by a local historical foundation's account. Business essentially ceased.

Out of Arcadia, doom drove Evangeline to Louisiana. To what ends of earth did ill winds blow Champagne's deported masses? Some fled back to Paris for a short-lived respite before being driven out yet again. What fates awaited the others?

The year 1307 brought yet more anguish to Champagne

The Knights of the Temple of King Solomon order – known as Templars – had formed around 1119 when Hugues de Payens of Champagne gathered eight relatives into a group to protect pilgrims on their journey to Jerusalem. In 1129 they became well-known in Europe after they were officially sanctioned at the Council of Troyes.

These warrior monks developed a banking system with drafts that were good at all Templar locations; they routinely used letters of credit to conduct business and possessed vast knowledge, from medicine to merchandise.

On Friday, 13th of October, 1307, the world awakened to the arrest of all Knights Templar; many were tortured and killed. The Knights Templar leader Jacques de Molay was burned at the stake. Their vast holdings in land and currency were confiscated.

Many questions about these times remain hanging.

Templar ties reached deep into Champagne

A short distance southeast of the town of Bar-sur-Aube – which had served as one of the locations of the medieval Champagne fairs – lies the valley where abbot Bernard of Clairvaux established a Cisterican abbey. An uncle of this abbot numbered among the original nine Knights Templar.

Cash, property and recruits flowed into the Knights' coffers at Bernard's bidding; Templars acquired extensive land holdings in Europe and the Middle East, including vineyards and farms. 1500 Templar houses and a fleet of ships counted among the Knights' assets.

Today in stark contrast to its formative stages, St. Bernard's abbey at Clairvaux is put to rough use. Within its walls it is no longer scholars who roam the hallowed halls, but incarcerated convicts.

From the 13th to the 15th century the region's rulers became ever more removed

Gone were the counts who fostered local prosperity; their successors acted to Champagne's deep detriment.

First Capetian domination drained its vitality. Jeanne de Navarre married Philippe IV le Bel in 1284, bringing with her a dowry of the Champagne region. Philippe IV's resultant rule as Count of Champagne ushered in a period of expulsions and massacres. As King of France it was he who ordered the arrest of the Knights Templar in 1307 and their subsequent annihilation.

In the wake of these atrocities Champagne continued to suffer setbacks. With the marriage of Catherine de France to Henry V of England, the 1420 Treaty of Troyes put the city under English rule, further favoring outside interests.

In 1429 the town of Troyes was restored to French rule after remarkable intervention by Jeanne d'Arc in ousting the English. Shortly thereafter she was burned at the stake.

In the centuries that followed, warfare, pestilence and religious upheavals countered the many efforts to recapture Champagne's former radiance.

Then came champagne

In the land that still held the legacy of textile fairs, new developments in winemaking took firm hold. Starting from solid white chalk the golden elixir flowed forth to induce forgetfulness and recall the glory days of yore.

Following behind the sword-wielding maid of Orléans, Champagne's 19th- and 20th-century women riddled, clarified and exported the potion that beguiled a ready world.

Exquisite textiles traded to the four corners of the medieval world may always remain enmeshed in Champagne's deep memories, but now a liquid form of enchantment flows from its portals to all points in graceful green glass.

The history

From soaring heights to plunging depths

The Champagne-Ardenne region and the various parts that comprise it have seen the best of times and the worst of times. They have seen the heights of collegiality and enterprise and the depths of villainy, conflict and greed. The following exposé highlights some of the events and personnages that have shaped Champagne's fate.

Roman roots

For more than a millennium, vineyards have formed part of the landscapes that would later become France. Early Greeks had seen Gaul in the first century BCE, at a time when it was essentially the size of present-day France and composed of scattered Celtic kingdoms. At that time historian Dioderus Siculus pronounced the area too cold and barren for either vines or olive trees to grow.

By the dawning of the current era until the mid 5th century Rome ruled most of Gaul. At that time Romans well understood various methods for planting, grafting, training and pruning of grape vines that by then had been widely used for a good 200 years in the sunnier parts of the empire, as reported by Cato the Censor (*De agri cultura*, 234–149 BCE).

Roman historian Justin claims that wine first had been introduced to Gaul by Greek settlers in Marseille (Massalia). In any case, amphorae of wine had reached Gaul long before Julius Caesar's soldiers did in 52 BCE.

By all indications, the wine trade spread quickly across the European Continent, enriching Roman merchants and spreading the taste for wine as a daily necessity in all social levels. By the first century of the current era the vines had become so popular that a decree that issued from Emperor Domitian ordered that they all be uprooted and replanted with basic food crops like corn. Apparently vineyards had become so plentiful that they had overtaken other forms of agriculture.

Accounts from that period indicate that Romans generally viewed viticulture as a boon of civilization on an order of magnitude with constitutional governance and urban life. Respected writers such Pliny the Elder described prized vintages and first growths, or grand cru, vineyards. Rome had already experienced a golden age in wine a century before invading Gaul; three centuries later Rome's provinces were regularly supplying Rome with wines produced in the provinces.

Historically the Champagne region had been considered too cold for red grapes to properly ripen and achieve the high sugar levels to rival its Burgundian neighbors' luscious rich red wines to the south. Adding another liability, Romans had heavily quarried its poor chalky terrain, leaving the lands deeply scarred.

A 5th-century coronation ignites a passion for champagne wines

Early in the 5th century Germanic Franks invaded Belgica, a Roman province west of the Rhine River frontier, and their warlord established his kingdom in Reims. After this Merovingian King Clovis was anointed, so the story goes, a lavish party ensued. The regional wine – a paltry, murky and distant contender with the famous rich red wines from its Burgundian neighbor to the south – nonetheless inspired the lifting of a glass of »champagne wine« by virtually all of the kings crowned in Reims after Clovis. (37 coronations took place in the cathedral there between 816 and 1825 alone.) At the time even St. Remi, who performed the honors for Clovis, owned vineyards himself.

Frankish territories expanded under Merovingian rule, which lasted from the mid 5th century until 752. It is generally thought that the duchy of Campania, as Champagne was then known, included civitates (settlements of Roman citizens) of Reims, Chalons-sur-Marne, Laon and Troyes.

Epernay becomes known for wines during 9th-century Carolingian Empire

The coronation of Charlemagne in Aix-la-Chapelle in 800 began the French realm of the early Middle Ages and the advent of the Holy Roman Empire. A revival of learning known as the Carolingian renaissance took place under Alcuin (c. 732–804), an Anglo-Latin poet, educator and cleric who, as head of the Palatine school established by Charlemagne at Aix-la-Chapelle, introduced traditions of Anglo-Saxon humanism into Western Europe. In 782 Charlemagne gave the Abbey of St. Loup to Alcuin; in the following century it reverted to the Counts of Champagne thus becoming a secular abbey.

From 850 until 1328 Champagne was ruled by counts, first of Troyes, then of Meaux and Troyes, and from 1022 onward by the Counts of Champagne. In 843 the Treaty of Verdun brought Troyes into the Kingdom of France under King Charles the Bald. By the time the Carolingian era ended in 888, the wines of Epernay had already earned special mention in written records.

Champagne's counts gain a Loire connection amid centuries of Capetian rule

The largest and oldest European royal house was founded by Hugh Capet (939–996) and descended from both Merovingian and Carolingian bloodlines. Capetian rule generally is cited as being from 987–1848, although with some interruptions.

In the 10th century ten years of turmoil resulted from the struggle for the Reims bishopric. Longer and worse, however, was the fight between Hugues Capet and Charles of Lorraine for the French throne, which also took place on Champagne soil. Four times within 60 years Reims found itself under attack and Epernay was besieged six times and burned twice. Hugues Capet sacked Epernay in the fall of 947, set fire to the entire area and stole all its wine. Eventually Herbert de Vermandois wrestled away the bishopric of Reims for his son and the house of Vermandois captured the title of Counts of Champagne. By 987 Hugues Capet's son and namesake was crowned King of France in Reims.

In the early 11th century on the death of Etienne, the Count of Troyes and Meaux, his cousin Eudes II, the Count of Blois, inherited Champagne. Thus

p. 6
1. Café scene on Place Drouet d'Erlon, Reims.

began a long – albeit interrupted – period of rule that pulled together the interests of the Loire Valley's Blois with Champagne lands.

At the death of Eudes II, Count of Champagne, in 1037, his lands were divided between his two sons. Etienne the Cadet took the counties of Troyes, Meaux and Vitry, while Thibaut the 1st took Blois, Tours, Chartres, Provins and St. Florentin.

Troyes and Blois joined forces against the French king when in 1041–44 Etienne de Troyes and Thibaut de Blois took part in a rebellion against King Henry the 1st. Thibaut 1st reunified Bleso-champenoise possessions, which continued when Etienne-Henri, then Thibaut II, inherited the counties of Blois and Meaux. Meanwhile Troyes, Vitry and Epernay were passed from Eudes IV to Hugues (1093).

Thus, in the late 11th century the county of Troyes evolved into Champagne. Especially after he assumed power in 1093, Hugues' undertakings in the Middle East brought notoriety to entire area of Champagne.

Until 1284, during the times in which the county of Champagne remained freer of the kingdom of France's control, the area was known for innovations in its judiciary processes. Sessions were held at Troyes as often as three times a year and, after the French parliament took its place more permanently in Paris in the middle of the 13th century, these judicial sessions became known as the »Jours de Troyes« or »dies Trecensis«. By the 14th century a distinction began to be made between matters of greater or lesser gravity – »Grands jours« or »magnus« for the higher courts.

The 12th- and 13th-century's illustrious Champagne fairs create a trade emporium

An early mention of a trade fair held in the Champagne region occurred in a 5th century letter between clerics. The next mention may not have occurred until 1100, and certainly at that time the fairs were renown and legendary. Although they probably started out as agricultural, their reach soon spread to textiles produced in the Champagne area, but also to products such as leather, fur and spices from increasingly further away.

By the 12th and 13th century they had attained a high level of sophistication; not to be conversant with the champagne fairs, as an expression, meant to be out of the loop.

Financing could cover a wide range of contingencies, and disputes could be settled quickly and locally. *Lex mercatoria*, a merchant law outside the realm of feudalism and based on the notion of keeping a good name, served the entire span between the Mediterranean and the northern climes. Those who did business at the fairs could be assured of security in their dealings; agreements were recognized and honored even outside the boundaries of Champagne. In around 1137 fair participants were granted safe passageway to and from the fairs, *conduit aux marchands*. (Later, in 1204, Philippe Auguste put the fairs under royal protection.) At the *banche* of Italian lenders, credit instruments and loan transactions developed easily and became commonplace, fueled by innovations in coinage and bookkeeping from southern spheres. The Troy ounce, *marc de troyes,* as a standard for measuring precious metals, is believed to derive from the fairs at Troyes, probably mid 12th century.

According to commonly held thought, six annual fairs each lasted several weeks, beginning in Lagny and ending in Troyes. After Lagny the fair moved to Bar-sur-Aube, to Provins for the »May fair«, to Troyes for the »hot fair« in late June, back to Provins in September, and then to Troyes for the final »cold fair«. During the first eight days the merchants set up their wares; then came the cloth fair and the leather fair, followed by the fair for spices and other goods that lent themselves to being weighed. The four days at the end were saved for settling of accounts.

Locations for the fairs followed Roman footsteps; each was situated at a longtime crossroads or stopping point. Troyes and Provins had served as Charlemagne's administrative headquarters. In Bar-sur-Aube the fair was held on the estate grounds of the Count of Champagne; in Provins it was held in the shadow of a church on the flatlands. Provins still maintains intact the *granges aux dimes*, a prototypical example of the Champagne fair's out-sized buildings with first floor spaces allotted to display and trade and miles of cellar tunnels for storage. Wares came to Champagne from Marseille, Germany, Spain, Sicily and North Africa on a regular basis.

The Champagne fairs rose in fame and fortune to become the center of international trade and finance, due to the combined efforts of the local church and state, most notably St. Bernard de Clairvaux and the Counts of Champagne.

In an odd reversal of effect, even an 1182 expulsion served to further Champagne's successes. Capetian King Philippe Auguste's banishment of Jewish merchants from his realm and confiscation of their lands caused the majority to relocate to the Champagne region. During his absence from the area from 1189 to 1192 while on the 3rd crusade in the Middle East, Marie of France (1145 to 1198), Countess of Champagne and Troyes, welcomed and protected the merchants. When Philippe returned and realized the consequences of his action, he ordered the »Royal Jews« back to Paris, where he built les Halles as the center of mercantile operations under the protection of royal guards.

It was not until 1710 that the last Champagne fairs were suppressed and relocated to Reims and Lyon, but by then their vitality had been dissipated hundreds of years before.

Champagne's 12th-century Knights Templar build a financial empire

In 1095 a man from Champagne, Pope Urbain II (Eudes de Lagery), issued an appeal to other men in the region to liberate Jerusalem from people he considered to be infidels. It is commonly thought that the motivation behind this action was to redirect the focus of garrulous local knights from fighting each other on home territory to instead attacking a foe on a more distant battleground. Urbain's call to arms was heeded by an overwhelming number of his fellows.

By spring of 1096 an unruly mob set out in the general direction of the Middle East, but on their way they attacked Jewish communities in the

Rhineland and Danube basin. In the years that followed, many more waves of motley mounted cavalry traversed the Bosporus Straits into Asia. The city of Constantinople, situated right in their path, was also ravaged in April, 1204, when the 4th crusade under the direction of Pope Innocent III, deviated from its intended Middle East destination and instead sacked and conquered the capital of the Eastern Roman Empire (Byzantium).

Until 1272, when the 9th crusade ended in failure, a series of religiously-driven military campaigns swept across a vast swath of lands between Europe and the Middle East, and included such disasters as the children's crusade in which thousands of men 15 years old and younger died or were sold into slavery, and the Albigensian crusade and inquisition of 1209, which was launched against a group called Cathars in the Languedoc area of what is now France, then known as Occitania. The Cathars were denounced as heretics for their beliefs inconsistent with Catholicism.

Once the crusaders had taken Jerusalem on July 15, 1099, they began to institute western feudal practices by installing a Latin church that was loyal to the pope in Rome. In 1119/20 Hugues, a knight from near Troyes in Champagne, and eight companions formed a group that called itself »the cavalry of the poor knights of Christ of the Temple of Salomon« (*templiers*, Knights Templar), charged with the protection and security of pilgrims coming to Jerusalem.

King Baldwin II of Jerusalem gave the Knights Templar a part of the palace that was on the esplanade of the temple, at the center of which had stood the temple of Solomon in times past, according to historian Guillaume de Tyr. This space became headquarters for an operation that grew in wealth, power, land holdings, military and financial expertise to the extent that it may have become a threat to both the church and state of medieval Europe. Information about specifics for this time period is scarce, sometimes limited to multi-hand accounts written long after the fact.

Names of Hugues' original fellow Templars were given as Godfrey de Saint-Omer, Payen de Montdidier, Archambaud de St. Agnan, Andre de Montbard, Geoffrey Bison, Rossal Gondamer, with the ninth possibly having been Hugues, the Count of Champagne. As Troyes served as Count Hugues' most important city and domain, it was also recognized as south Champagne's capital. When Hugues became a Templar in 1125, he left the county of Champagne to his nephew Thibaut II of Blois.

The three orders that arose out of the chaos – priests, knights and peasants – also introduced the new concept of associating clerics with combat. Although scholars of this period often attribute the annihilation of the Templars to the fact that the French king was so financially indebted to them, the Knights' superlative strength in so many regards, particularly military, may have proven as great a factor.

For the most part the crusader knights consisted of free men, but undisciplined, quarrelsome and violent, barely restrained even from pillaging their own churches on Sunday, Christmas and Easter. The warrior monks went beyond the ordinary crusader to assume long-term vows that combined the ascetic life of monasteries with their militaristic mission. The Templars were also exhorted by King Baldwin II to seek out more recruits, which they did in Champagne, Anjou, Normandy, Picardie, Languedoc, Provence, Flanders, England, Scotland and Spain. In the process they developed an impressive international following.

The crusades and its various ramifications depleted Champagne of its men and prompted the growth of its vineyards in order to finance the effort. Commonly those who answered the call to take their sword and horse to the Middle East left their lands to the church. The monks then were charged with tending the farms and vineyards; wine became ever more important in welcoming visitors and as part of the clerical rituals.

Around the year 1130 St. Bernard de Clairvaux, founder of the Cistercian order, published a letter in praise of the new knighthood, garnering increased support, especially from the church. St. Bernard, a relative of Hugues, drew up the Latin Rule as the governing code of behavior for the Templars. In 1139 the Council of Troyes issued a *bulle omne* that gave considerable rights to the Templars, substantially increasing their strength in the Middle East and Europe.

Upon becoming Count of Champagne Thibaut IV (le Grand, 1090–1152) continued his uncle Hugues' support of the Cistercians. By 1144 under St. Bernard's leadership the Cistercians had rapidly expanded to 350 monasteries, with its abbey at Clairvaux situated just south of Troyes in the heart of Champagne country. St. Bernard's backing for both the Champagne fairs and its warrior knights buoyed the status and prestige of both, but put him at ever greater risk as both achieved seemingly boundless success in places removed from both Rome and Paris.

During the 20 year period from about 1160 to 1180 the Middle Ages achieved a pinnacle of literary and artistic accomplishment. This marked the age of poets, troubadours, and writers, especially Chrétien de Troyes, who authored *Eric and Enide* (1170), and sagas about Yvain and Lancelot.

Generally considered to have been weak leaders, Capetian kings ruled France during the early crusades. For a time Champagne sat as an island of calm at the crossroads. Those traveling from the North Sea to the Mediterranean or between Frankish and Germanic lands could rely on its respite once they reached Champagne.

By the 1200s events had turned tumultuous. Thibaut IV fought with the king of France against the English, but abandoned and then was accused of having poisoned him. The county of Champagne was invaded, and Thibaut IV granted charters to his towns of Troyes, Provins, Vitry, Epernay, Sézanne and Vertus. He became King of Navarre, joined the revolt of barons against Blanche of Castille and then submitted to the French crown in 1236. He had 183 Cathars burned as heretics on Champagne's Mont Aimé.

In the early Middle Ages Champagne's courts had been run directly by counts of Champagne until Thibaut IV became King of Navarre in 1234 and essentially relocated to Spain leaving surrogates in charge. From then on the counts of Champagne ostensibly maintained control from half a continent away.

On the broader scene the pope authorized inquisitions and torture in 1252, and the Mongols took Baghdad in 1258.

A 13th-century dowry leads to decades of wide-ranging skullduggery

In one of the greatest ironies of history, the ruler responsible for perhaps the greatest atrocities in Champagne's past was named »the Beautiful«. Philippe le Bel (the IV, 1268–1314) donned the monarch's crown at a very young age and, during his short life, reputedly was responsible for the untold numbers of deaths, including popes and Templars, and massive confiscations and expulsions and ultimately the demise of the Champagne fairs. How these events came to be has been a subject of much research and debate. Obscurity continues to reign, but intrigue plays a commanding role.

In 1284, when 16-year-old Philippe le Bel married 13-year-old Jeanne (1271–1305), control of Champagne passed into the boy's hands as part of Jeanne's dowry as heiress of Champagne. A 1275 treaty between Jeanne's mother Blanche of Artois and Philippe le Bel's father, King Philippe III, had mandated that Blanche's daughter Jeanne marry one of King Philippe III's older sons. Accordingly, mother Blanche had handed over her toddler Jeanne to the king's household. In 1285, just one year after their marriage, the teenage couple became King and Queen of France. King Philippe III had died on the way back from an unsuccessful crusade against Aragon, a medieval kingdom in northeastern Spain.

For the 20 years that followed, while aged 17 to 37, King Philippe le Bel wreaked havoc on Champagne as well as his entire French kingdom.

Jacques de Molay, head of the Templars in 1296, took the part of Boniface VIII against Philippe le Bel. In 1302 the Council of Rome issued a bull against Philippe le Bel. In 1306 Philippe IV confiscated Jewish property. On Friday 13, 1307, he arranged for the arrest of all Templars in the kingdom. A 1308 papal bull by Clement V ordered all princes to arrest the Templars in their realms. Within the following two years 54 templiers were burned at the stake.

By secret process Clement V approved the suppression of the Order of the Temple in 1312 and directed that all their possessions and holdings be delivered to the Ordre de l'hôpital. In 1314 Jacques de Molay was burned at the stake and the templiers were absorbed by the hospitaliers.

In 1328 the last son of Philippe le Bel died without heir, marking the end of the Capetian dynasty.

From 1346 to 1353 Europe was beset by the black plague.

Dark clouds follow the death of Jeanne d'Arc in the 15th century

In 1417 Troyes had become the provisional capital of the French kingdom, but fell under English rule under a 1420 treaty. The marriage that took place in Troyes between Catherine of France and Henry V that same year resulted in the disinheritance of young dauphin Charles VII.

In 1429 Troyes was restored to French rule after Jeanne d'Arc, the maid of Orléans, helped oust the English. In 1431 she was captured in Compiègne, sold to the English and led to Rouen where she was burned at the stake.

1517 brought pestilence, 1524 the great fire of Troyes. The Seine flooded repeatedly.

By the 16th century one pope and three kings owned some of Champagne's vines. Although far from its refined style of today, an intense-tasting but still pale and cloudy champagne was the only wine served at the coronation of Henri III in 1575.

The 17th century brings innovations by Dom Pérignon

Although many accounts attribute to Dom Pérignon (1638–1715) the major inventions related to the development of champagne in its current form, these feats may have been somewhat skewed by a major advertising campaign that took place in the meantime. The monk and cellar master at the Benedictine abbey in Hautvillers sought unsuccessfully to remove from the wine unsightly, big bubbles known as toad's eyes, *yeux de crapauds*, that were considered to be the mark of poor winemaking from having spent too much time in the cask. The expression commonly attributed to him: »Come quickly, I am tasting the stars!« may have romanticized his actual contributions.

Indisputably, however, he is credited for initiating the practice of blending the must, or unfermented juice, from different vintages, or years of harvest, in order to achieve a specific taste. He also used hemp to tie down the cork to the bottle, and made thicker glass bottles to prevent explosions. However, most authorities agree that he was not the primary innovator of sparkling wines, since that degree of refinement did not take place until the 19th century. Regardless of particulars, Dom Pérignon is considered by all to have been a leading light in the history of champagne, an extraordinary vintner who advanced the knowledge of viticulture and enology.

From the mid 17th century the regions of Champagne and Burgundy had been engaged in lively discussions over the superiority of their respective wines and by the 18th century it was resolved in an unexpected way. Once Champagne winemakers devised a way to keep the bubbles in their wines and the wines in their bottles, the health benefits that were suddenly attributed to their bubbly wines pushed champagne's popularity to the heights. No longer did it matter whose wine was better – both Burgundy's rich red wines and Champagne's sparkling ones were exceptional in their own rights.

Still the conundrum persisted into the 19th century: how to both encourage and contain fine bubbles. The frequency of exploding glass kept decades of winery workers wearing shatterproof glasses while the inconsistency of the occurrence and size of the bubbles made production unreliable. Still red and white wines accounted for 90% of champagne wine production as of the late 18th century.

Although it is tempting to limit the discussion of champagne's development to the Champagne region, it should be noted that the English appear to have contributed as well. According to some sources, although monks had produced sparkling wine in the Carcassonne area of France as early as the 1530s, scientific advances in the production had taken place in England about a century later. Later still, in the second half of the 17th century England of Charles II, accounts tell of wine shipped by cask and bottled by English aristocrats, with the addition of a spot of sugar to enhance the sparkle.

18th-century French Revolution sets governing changes into motion

The absolute monarchy that had ruled France for centuries collapsed in the late 1700s. Parliament was exiled to Troyes in 1787; the Bastille fell July 14, 1789. The citizens' declaration of rights was issued on August 26, 1789.

In 1790 the department of the Aube was created.

A constitutional republic existed from 1795 to 1799. 1799–1815 marked the Napoleonic Era. During his campaign against Russia, Napoléon made Troyes the base of his operations and signed the victory at Brienne-le-Château in the Aube, where he had resided from 1779 to 1784 while he studied at the military academy.

During the Napoleonic Wars that raged between 1803 and 1815, champagne makers discovered that they could substitute beet sugar for cane sugar and grow the sugar beets themselves. Prior to that time champagne production had been interrupted whenever shipments of cane sugar from the West Indies colonies failed to reach France. Sugar mills were quickly built in the area to process the beets right in the vicinity, thus avoiding shipping problems altogether. More plants were added just after World War II.

The Bourbon restoration lasted from 1814 to 1830; the July Monarchy from 1830 to 1848. Napoléon III ruled from 1848 to 1871.

In the late 19th century phylloxera wreaked havoc in Europe and especially in France, and destroyed most of the vineyards. These tiny sap-sucking relatives of the aphid devastated France's wine production. Ultimately vines were grafted onto disease-resistant root stock imported from California, a practice that continues to be successful in thwarting the pest.

As a consequence of the phylloxera outbreak and beginning in about 1908, vintners began relying on grapes grown beyond the original boundaries of the »champagne« designation, most notably the Aube region just to the south. The dissention about where the boundary lines should be drawn gave rise to the revolt in 1911 by growers in the Aube. The departments as drawn in 1927 in response to the turmoil remain in effect today: the Aube, the Marne, the Aisne, the Haute-Marne and the Seine-et-Marne.

Phylloxera, known in California as a root louse, had attacked the few vineyards in the Napa Valley in the late 1800s, forcing vintners to plant new vines and devise methods that could withstand the onslaught. Both the experience from combatting the pest in Napa and the importation of root stock from California's vintners served the Champagne region well in overcoming the problem in France.

19th-century innovations

The early 1800s saw many innovations in champagne production: wine muzzles and corking machines, sugar ratios for the second fermentation. In 1840 Adolphe Hacquesson patented *muselet*, the wire and cork apparatus for securing the bottle closure, and the *capsulets*, the little metal lids.

Also in this time period Jean-Baptiste François devised a measure for residual sugar called *réduction François* or *dosage*, thus reducing breakages and allowing better control of the effervescence. From the days of Dom Pérignon it was commonly known that the sweeter grapes produced greater quantities of alcohol and carbonic acid, but this breakthrough allowed vintners to greatly refine the process.

Bottle labels then also began listing appellation, name of the producer, and other particulars.

20th-century arts, parks and science

The Third Republic and the Belle Epoque ran from 1871 until the beginning of World War I in 1914. This period gave rise to the sensuous style of the Belle Epoque; Art Nouveau captured the imagination of champagne drinkers with its elegant portrayals of the fair sex and its light whimsical touch. Against all odds and despite some of the worst of times, the best vintage year ever in the Champagne region's history occurred in 1914. World War I raged. Men who would have harvested the grapes had gone to fight in the war; women and children who had been left behind held together the operations. Conditions above ground were filled with gunfire and hostile troops. Underground they nursed the war-wounded, held school classes and pressed the grapes.

In 1935 *Appellation d'Origine Controlée* system instituted the notion of »terroirs«, that a wine derives its unique character from where the grapes are grown. At that time hundreds of appellations were identified that have grown to about 450 currently. Strict rules set the type of grapes, yields per hectare, minimum maturity of the grapes defined by the sugar content, and the percentage of alcohol. In Champagne regulations require that the grapes be hand-picked.

The following year, 1936, saw the formation of le Front Populaire government after its victory in legislative elections. Three years later World War II began: in 1940 German forces seized Troyes; in 1944 the Allies invaded Normandy. Troyes and the Aube were liberated by American troops under General Patton.

The 1970s park creation era

The Parc naturel régional de la Forêt d'Orient was formed to the east of Troyes in 1970; the Parc naturel régional de la Montagne de Reims in 1976. The role of the parks in the Champagne region, discussed more fully below in the parks section, has been to help maintain the landscape and to encourage an ecological balance in the area, as well as to provide open space, agricultural and recreational opportunities. A wider effect has been felt throughout the world as large champagne producers fanned out to find conditions similar to those in the Champagne region.

In 1973, for example, Moët & Chandon numbered among several champagne houses in researching California's Napa Valley. Moët had spent two years before it settled on Napa as a good choice, then quietly began acquiring land in the central and southern valley. While waiting for its own vineyards to mature, Moët bought grapes from and used the facillities of the Trefethen family winery. In the main building, which had originally housed the former Eschol winery – two separate operations shared the space: Trefethen Vineyards on the ground floor and Moët's subsidiary Domaine Chandon on the level above.

Another cooperative effort between France and California is said to have led to the improvement in champagne's second fermentation, which also occurred around the year 1973. A California winemaker had devised the method for converting malic acid into lactic acid, giving the wine a smoother taste. Apparently the lab at Beaulieu vineyard had produced the starter which was then used successfully at Souverain and Mondavi wineries and ultimately proved especially beneficial in the second fermentation for champagne making.

Champagne's illustrious widows

Strong hands, soft touches

19th and 20th century women transformed the champagne trade. Places of work became more welcoming, in appearance and in function; guests were received graciously at the champagne houses. Language relating to champagne making stayed close to home – champagne »house«, »gateau«, »chapeau«.

The following section is devoted to five women whose lives span 200 years exactly. When faced with adversity they not only prevailed but excelled, and made champagne and Champagne, in large part, what they are today. These phenomenal widows followed each other about 40 years apart, except for the last two who lived in roughly the same era. Barbe-Nicole Ponsardin (»Veuve Clicquot«) was born in 1777 and Elizabeth Law de Lauriston-Boubers (»Madame Jacques«) died in 1977.

In Reims, a city richly laden with a storied past, memories of two of these widows in particular remain finely woven into the city's fabric. Both left landmarks that attest to the extent of their innovative achievements. Commanding the stage at two different points in history, each built legacies that continue to reflect their style and extraordinary successes. The innovative contributions of all five women to both the art and science of champagne shaped the trade.

In Reims still today vestiges of their lives evidence both their generosity and the esteem in which they are still regarded by that city. Although Veuve Clicquot's influence reached deep into the 20th century, without doubt the greatest impact was reserved for the first to follow her, Jeanne Pommery. As a young mother, suddenly widowed in a world that had been dominated exclusively by men, Veuve Clicquot set an example that up until that time had been unknown and unimaginable. By the time 39 year-old Jeanne Pommery abruptly lost her husband Louis-Alexandre in 1858, the Veuve Clicquot already had built an internationally-known commercial empire as well as a philanthropic legacy.

Barbe-Nicole Clicquot (1777–1866)

Barbe-Nicole Ponsardin had not set out to revolutionize the wine industry. Raised in an influential family with a textile manufacturing business and political ties, she learned at an early age how to keep a low profile during uncertain times.

Madame Ponsardin's great-grandfather Nicolas Ruinart – another now famous name in the champagne trade – had been the nephew of Dom Thierry Ruinart, a colleague of winemaking legend Dom Pérignon. Dom Pérignon allegedly passed his secrets in winemaking to Dom Thierry, who in turn whispered them to his nephew Nicolas, who then in 1729 founded Ruinart, the world's first champagne house.

Barbe-Nicole had started out life as a privileged little girl. Her father Ponce-Jean-Nicolas Ponsardin headed a rich industrial family that dealt in woolens, the renown commodity from that area at the time. Her well-connected father also had been appointed as mayor of Reims, and had received heads of state that included King Louis XVI when he was consecrated in the Reims cathedral, Napoléon Bonaparte and his wife Joséphine on their triumphal return from Belgium and the newly crowned Marie-Louise of Austria. Within their local realm he gained popularity by setting up the first chamber of commerce and instituted measures to help the unfortunate and jobless populations in Reims.

In her twelfth year, that glamorous life had changed dramatically for Barbe-Nicole. During the years that followed, the region underwent periods of revolution, the fall of the empire and the return of the monarchy.

Barbe-Nicole had been studying at a convent school in an abbey where many wealthy young women had been educated, Marie Stuart among them. The abbey started to become an object of political contention, and was later sold. Mindful of danger brewing, Barbe-Nicole's father sent her into the countryside to live with a trusted seamstress for a number of years, where she was clothed in humble attire and pretended to be a member of that family.

Ponce Ponsardin managed to navigate through periods of revolution, the fall of an empire and the return of the royalty with his affairs remarkably intact. As trouble began to brew before fighting broke out in 1789, he joined the Jacobins, or »sans culottes (»without pants«, the implication being »without a rich man's pants«), a radical fringe group that advocated social change and ultimately brought about the French Revolution. It was not until after the fall of Robespierre that Barbe-Nicole came back to Reims to rejoin her family in the Hôtel Ponsardin, built by her father in 1780 and which now houses the city's chamber of commerce. Here she continued her studies, although then under preceptors who came to her quarters where she led a discrete and withdrawn existence.

When she reached the age of 20 she met 23-year-old François-Marie Clicquot, who had been sent away to Switzerland by his family during the turbulent years to study the German language and financing. They were married in a secret ceremony attended only by close family in the underground cellars below the Hôtel Ponsardin, dug many centuries before by Romans quarrying chalk deposits. Her father also provided her with a generous dowry that included a number of prime properties in the Champagne region.

After he was married, François-Marie Clicquot began to concentrate all his efforts in his father's wine business, which until then had been a minor sideline of the main banking and cloth merchandising concerns. In those days both François and his new bride could often be seen together in their horse-drawn carriage visiting the Montagne de Reims (a prime pinot noir grape-growing region that now belongs to the Parc naturel régional de la Montagne de Reims), the Vallée de la Marne and the Côte des Blancs, the three regions now considered to be the best places to grow pinot noir, pinot meunier and chardonnay grapes respectively. Eager to learn all aspects of the business, François delved into the caves to converse with the winemakers, learned the methods of cultivation and negotiated the purchase of grapes.

François wanted his superb champagnes to grace all the royal tables of Europe – especially czarist Russian – and he saw the whole world as his market. In furtherance of these goals he began making initial trips to Switzerland, Germany and Austria where along the way he met a young Rhinelander who eventually would effectuate his plans, but long after Francois' death. Louis Bohne eventually promoted Clicquot champagnes in England, Prussia, Poland, Italy, Holland, but his greatest feat occurred in Russia on the heals of Napoléon's devastating defeat there.

On that horrible day in 1805 when a fever apparently took the life of François, however, Barbe-Nicole could have had no notion of what the future would hold. Her father-in-law, distraught by the death of his son, would have sold off all his business ventures if Veuve Clicquot had not pleaded with him to let her have the champagne sector. Although she had no training other than what she had seen while accompanying her husband around their vineyards, she felt determined to continue his work. Despite strong objections to a woman taking on a man's affairs – coming even from within her family – she remained resolute.

Just before his death, François was known to have felt great disappointment because of the clashes between Napoléon and Russia's Czar Alexander I, seeing politics threaten his dreams of the international market. Indeed, during the first years when the business was under Veuve Clicquot's direction, Europe was ravaged by the Napoleonic Wars. Despite the uncertain times, however, within the first four months after her husband's death, she made the key move of engaging an expert in the field of choosing and blending wines, changing the name of the firm to reflect the addition: Veuve Clicquot Ponsardin, Fourneaux and Co. Her father-in-law furnished a large part of the funds for the venture and never regretted it.

In her inspections of all the processes involved in preparing a bottle of champagne for market, she became concerned about the delays and variation in quality brought about by sediments. Until that point wine from that region had been beset both by a murkiness that clouded the brownish pink substance and by big bubbles that could not be contained. Despite sarcasm from her employees, she doggedly pursued ways to improve the process. With help from her cellar master Antoine de Muller, she brought a door down into the cellars, cut holes into it and then stuck the bottles upside-down into the holes. By regularly turning the bottles a quarter turn she was able to collect the sediment in the neck of the bottle and then disgorge it, replacing the volume with a dose of sugared spirits or sweetened wine. Once she made this discovery, the entire industry embraced the method, greatly speeding and improving the production of champagne.

Following Napoléon's defeat in 1814, Reims became the battleground for the last fighting. Soldiers invaded the champagne cellars, ostensibly preferring the sounds of uncorking champagne bottles to that of cannon fire. The Veuve Clicquot's thinking was encapsulated by her words »Let them drink. They'll pay.«

Even before the French troops left the Russian front, a ship bearing 10,000 bottles of Veuve Clicquot champagne set sail for Russia and it arrived the very day that Russia reopened its borders to French trade. Even before the bottles ran out, Veuve Clicquot had sent another 20,000 bottles to St. Petersburg, forbidding the ship's captain to carry any bottles but hers. The reaction of the Russians was summed up by author Alexander Pushkin: »Un vin béni des dieux.« Veuve Clicquot had conquered Russia by peaceful means.

Other markets quickly opened, most notably England. As her business mushroomed, she associated another young man of German origin, Edouard Werlé, and gradually retreated to her vacation home to organize balls and grand dinners, as well as helping the poor, beginning a workers' retirement home, creating an emergency fund, and financing the restoration of the Roman artifact in Reims, the Porte de Mars.

In the crossing of the stars of two of the most important women to champagne's history, the Ponsardin family also owned land in what was then known as Chigny-la-Montagne, and more recently called Chigny-les-Roses in honor of another of its most famous widows, Louise Pommery. A one-time officer for Louis XV, Allart de Maisonneuve had planted vineyards on this southern side of the Montagne de Reims and the grapes from that *clos*, or walled enclosure, had quickly gained notice for their exceptional quality. The Cattier family, who still own a family champagne house in Chigny-les-Roses, is said to have grown grapes in Chigny at least since 1763, and they came into the ownership too of the Allart vineyards, the Clos du Moulin. Now much of the area in Montagne de Reims reputedly produces the finest pinot noir grapes. These vineyards just south of the city of Reims are protected by the constraints imposed by the Parc naturel régional de la Montagne de Reims.

As the Veuve Clicquot advanced in years, another bright feminine star arose to take champagne to new heights in a different direction. Jeanne Alexandrine Louise Mélin (1819–1890) invented the dry brut champagne. Up until that time champagne wines had tasted about ten times sweeter than today's demi-sec champagne, often containing 200 grams of residual sugar per bottle. The finest wines from the region had a brownish pink, due in part to the brandy that was added to the sugar syrup before the final corking. The reddish color came from the red grape skins that had been allowed to stain the must. People at the time commonly described champagne as grey – *gris*

2. Barbe-Nicole Clicquot-Ponsardin, the Veuve Clicquot.

de perle – and made with only the black pinot meunier or pinot noir grapes.

Jeanne Alexandrine Mélin Pommery (1819 to 1890)

The stunning example of Veuve Clicquot's champagne empire must have shone brightly to Jeanne Alexandrine Mélin Pommery (1819–1890) when she was suddenly thrust into widowhood in 1858 at age 39. Like Veuve Clicquot she had been raised in a family of wealthy landowners. By that time her husband Louis Alexandre Pommery, who specialized in the Reims woolen trade, had bought a former prison where he stored his skeins in the underground cells. He also had befriended Narcisse Greno, founder of a small champagne firm.

Upon the retirement of M. Greno's partner in 1856, the business had become »Pommery et Greno«; wool soon replaced bottles in Louis' subterranean spaces. An influx of capital had bolstered the firm's finances when two short years later Louis unexpectedly passed away leaving Jeanne with a 17-year-old son and one-year-old daughter. At the time Jeanne, like the famous widow before her, had no expertise with either champagne or business.

Like Veuve Clicquot, Jeanne Pommery had the good fortune of devoted colleagues. Narcisse Greno, distraught by his partner's demise, pleaded with the widow to succeed her husband and promised his continued involvement – including as travelling salesperson – for the following four years. A brother of one of Veuve Pommery's classmates also remained with the firm as collaborator and administrator extraordinaire.

During those days the Russian trade was most highly coveted. Veuve Clicquot's champagnes had been favored for their sweetness, and since the time of Dom Pérignon, sugar had been added as part of the dosage that came after bottling. Veuve Pommery recognized that this very sweet rendition of champagne condemned it to be regarded only as a dessert wine – a drink for the ladies.

Veuve Pommery had quickly become an accomplished taster – from the grapes on the vine to the fermented, disgorged, aged, bottled, bubbly elixir and all along the way inbetween. She began to experiment by separating out a small amount of champagne to which no or very little sugar had been added. Then she convened a group of friends to try it. They first reacted with surprise, then denounced it as »hard«, but by the second glass all of them had been won over by the charm, agreeability and lightness of it. Thus »brut« was born.

Moving champagne away a dessert drink meant freeing it to be sipped at any hour. This monumental change in the way champagne was enjoyed enabled the successive and successful widow Bollinger to famously later say: »I drink it when I'm happy and when I'm sad. I drink it sometimes when I'm alone. When I'm not I consider it obligatory. In other circumstances, I never touch it, except when I'm thirsty.«

England became Veuve Pommery's favored clientele. As a young woman she had spent a year studying in England; she readily opened a London office in 1861. At this point too her innovative spirit came through. As orders flooded from across the Channel, Veuve Pommery found that she needed more storage space; her brut champagnes required longer periods of aging.

»Outside the walls« to the southeast of Reims she bought a vast valley, »les Crayères«, known for its extensive systems of underground tunnels. The Romans had quarried the chalk in the area to build their city of Durocortum, and successors had followed suit. Reims had been destroyed and rebuilt five or six times over the course of the centuries; these subterranean passageways had afforded shelter and secrecy during and construction materials after periods of conflicts.

One of the most trying times for Veuve Pommery occurred just as she finished the installation of the bottles into these newly acquired cellars. In 1870 the Franco-Prussian War broke out, followed by the capitulation of Napoléon III, on the heals of which came the entry of 30,000 to 40,000 Prussian soldiers into Reims. For almost two years some 5,500 Prussians occupied the city. On top of that, the harvest that year proved anemic and most of her collaborators and workers joined the army, while locals were left housing the enemy.

Over the advice of her friends who urged her to retreat to her country house in Chigny – that now belongs to the Parc naturel régional de la Montagne de Reims – and wait out the war, she stood firm and faced the onslaught with a dignity and steadfastness that gained respect from both sides. Multiple times she intervened on behalf of those who had been condemned to the firing squad or expulsion. Three doctors, one of whom later became the mayor of Reims, owed their reprieve directly to her efforts for them.

Once the war had passed, Veuve Pommery engaged in massive improvements in her operation, both above ground and below. On her numerous trips to England and Scotland she had become enamored with the 16th century Gothic style, to which she added Elizabethan touches with towers, turrets, donjons and crenelations and English gardens. Whimsy lifted the look of her winery into the sphere of bubbles and brut; inside artwork advanced the world of Art Nouveau, even down to the poster and label design.

A year later her 1874 *Brut Millésime* supply outsold and spread her fame to the Indies, the Far East and even America, which started to take a interest in champagne after the war. Even so, her routine continued as before: up at 5 a.m., personal attention to the vintners, blending, agents, principal clients, critiques and suggestions as well as tasting, often with friends. A passionate supporter of the arts – the Art Nouveau movement in particular benefited from her influence – she commissioned bas-reliefs to be hung in the caves and encouraged local artists by buying their best work. In 1890 she won over any detractors by purchasing *Des Glaneuses* by Jean-François Millet and donating it to the Louvre; today the painting hangs in the Musée d'Orsay.

Following Veuve Clicquot's philanthropic example, Veuve Pommery aided societies of music, gymnastics, an orphanage, children in poverty, as well as providing well for her own employees with good salaries, medical assistance, emergency help, and participating personally in their family events. Her own birthday was celebrated each year as a holiday when work – but not pay – was suspended in the cellars.

When she fell sick in 1889, she transferred many of her responsibilities to her son Louis, as she had in 1875 to her daughter Louise's new husband, the Marquis de Polignac, and in 1885 to her faithful companion since her first hours of widowhood, Henri Vasnier. In 1890 she died at the age of 71.

In 1907 the business passed to her grandson Melchoir de Polignac, who created a sports park that continues to be well used and loved by Reims, the Parc Pommery. Although the champagne house has passed into other hands since then, her great-great grandson continues in her tradition as the master of blending and vintages. In honor of her passion for roses the town of Chigny, where her country house was located, changed its name to Chigny-les-Roses.

Mathilde Emilie Laurent-Perrier (1852–1925)

In addition to Veuve Pommery, two other famous widows followed in the footsteps of the Veuve Clicquot. Widowed at age 35 in 1887 when her husband died in a freak accident while demonstrating new equipment to visitors, Mme. Laurent-Perrier was left with three children aged 14, 8 and 7. She ran the firm for 38 years through 1925, and found particular success in England.

Sharing with widows Veuve and Pommery the advantage of being born into a wealthy family, Mathilde Emilie Perrier was the daughter of a grower who after the French Revolution had bought extensive lands that had belonged to the diocese of Reims and Chalons-sur-Marne. Both she and her husband Eugène Laurent, whom she married in 1871, came from the small town of Tours-sur-Marne. There in a small house of champagne Eugène worked as head of the cellars »Le Roy et Pierlot«. In 1881 politics broke the partnership between le Roy, predictably the fervent royalist, and Pierlot the progressive spirit. When Pierlot died in 1881 at age 69, he left his entire business to Eugène.

Within the following six years Eugène bought a number of other vineyards in the terroirs of Tourssur Marne, Bouzy and Ambonnay, all prime pinot noir grape-growing areas that are now part of the Parc naturel régional de la Montagne de Reims. He also dug new extensive new cellars, as well as renovating existing facilities and equipment. Following his sudden death his widow continued the renovations, gaining credibility from creditors by using life insurance proceeds to pay off existing debts.

English clients in particular appreciated her champagne and she entertained them lavishly. Her daughter and granddaughter would later describe her as »authoritative – you didn't dare butt heads with her« – and avid about gardening and education. A hands-on administrator, she directed with fierce determination and constant presence, while still lunching every day with her daughter, accompanying her granddaughter to see the peacocks and golden pheasants and collect eggs. At 4 p.m. each day she drank a blanc-de-blanc champagne, made only from the grapes of her favorite hill, specially produced for her in half bottles.

In 1911 when part of the region was sacked as part of a revolt, her workers spirited away treasures and furnishings from her estate and hid them in safe keeping until the danger of looting passed. In World War I, when Tours-sur-Marne found itself close to the front lines, she was gone from the area a total of only eight days in 1914, vowing to give the church a statue of Jeanne d'Arc if her village was spared. The statue remains there today.

Elisabeth Law de Lauriston-Boubers Bollinger (1899–1977)

Elisabeth Law de Lauriston-Boubers came from the Touraine region of France, part of the Paris basin of the Loire and its tributaries, an area also known for its viticulture. Once she married her husband Jacques-Joseph-Jacob-Placide Bollinger at age 24 and moved to the old Roman town of Aÿ, however, she donned the mantel of Champenoise. Elisabeth descended from the brother of renown Scottish financier, John Law, who had served as Controller General under King Louis XV; Jacques' great grandfather had been born in 1803 in the part of Germany that was the independent kingdom of Württemberg.

Jacques' ancestor had learned the champagne trade by working in a firm founded by Antoine Muller, a Bavarian who spent twelve years as chef de cave for Veuve Clicquot. Through these associations the Bollinger family had become acquainted with and eventually married into the family of a certain count Athanase-Louis-Emmanuel de Villermont who owned vineyards in the best terroirs of the champagne region: Aÿ, Bouzy, Cuis, and Verzenay. By the time Jacques inherited what had become the thriving Bollinger family business that had been passed down from generation to generation, the house had already received a Royal Warrant from Queen Victoria in 1884, making it the official supplier to the British court.

For her part, Elisabeth eagerly embraced the champagne trade, having grown up in a wine-growing region and having heard about the stunning breakthroughs and successes that had been taking place in the champagne industry. She and Jacques had been married for 18 years when Jacques died at the age of 47 in 1941. In World War I he had won the Légion d'honneur award for his work as an aviator. In World War II he was called up as a reserve, but was too sick to serve. He had returned to Aÿ at that time where he became mayor of his native town while it was fully occupied by German troops.

When Jacques died in 1941, Elisabeth at age 42 found herself alone at the head of an enterprise to which she was deeply attached and which she didn't want to see fail. She seized control with determination and vigor at a time when France was fully at war, and led the company for the next 31 years. Finding help in the vineyards and cellars became increasingly difficult; many from the region had been taken prisoners or sent to forced labor camps in Germany. Veuve Bollinger helped her employees and nursed the wounded.

If there is an iconic image of »Madame Jacques« or »Tante Lily«, as she was affectionately and widely known, it must be the one riding a bicycle through her vineyards and forest-clad hills in high heeled but sensible shoes and handsome suit. Each day in rain cape or sundress she surveyed her domain, from the planting to the picking and

3. Elisabeth Law de Lauriston-Boubers Bollinger on a bicycle inspecting her vineyards. (From: Serena Sutcliffe, *Champagne: The History and Character of the World's Most Celebrated Wine*, Simon and Schuster, New York, 1988, p. 88.)

press. At tastings she signaled her approval or lack thereof by a slightly raised eyebrow or a pout, leaving no doubt whether to include the Avize 1928 or the Bouzy 1964 in that year's blend.

Once the war ended, she led the company into a great expansion while resolutely holding to traditional techniques of wine-making: the first fermentation continued exclusively in oak casks. Having been raised under the care of an English governess, she spoke a perfect Shakespearian English, and used it to her advantage in her many trips to Britain, including the one as the first woman invited to attend the annual »Wine and Spirit Trade Society« in London. 1100 male colleagues gave her a long standing ovation.

In 1971 she relinquished her role to her nephews d'Hautefeuille and Bizot, and celebrated at a retirement banquet to which current and retired employees were invited. Since then »Bolly«, as it is called in England, continues to be family run and traces its roots proudly back to 1829 when it was founded in Aÿ by Hennequin de Villermont, Paul Renaudin and Jacques Bollinger. The Bollinger family itself claims roots in the Champagne region stretching back to 1585 when the Hennequins owned land in Cramant, a village just south of Aÿ.

Camille Olry-Roederer (1892–1975)

Special mention must be made here of another almost 20th century grand dame of champagne, who lived roughly at the same time as Elisabeth Bollinger. Camille Olry-Roederer took over the helm after her husband Léon Olry-Roederer died in 1932, and steered the company with a steady hand for the following 40 years.

In 1776 the firm was initially founded as Dubois Père & Fils. In the early 1800s it was run by a a man known as Schrieder (or Schroeder) who bequeathed the business to his nephew Louis Roederer in 1833 who then renamed it to Roederer.

Until Louis Roederer took over the firm, the Russian market had been dominated by Veuve Clicquot, Moët and Ruinart champagne houses. Within three years the Czar Alexander II himself was drinking Roederer champagnes and sending his emissary to Reims to act as his personal taster. According to legend, the special »cristal« bottles were made so that the czar would drink from bottles superior to his subjects. The crystal bottles – which at first were actually made from real crystal – had the additional advantage of being flat on the bottom rather than with the usual »punt« or dimple, apparently to eliminate the possibility of bombs being planted there.

When World War I broke out, almost three quarters of Roederer's champagnes were being sent to Russia. The firm almost went bankrupt when its shipments were blocked. By redirecting their efforts to the United States, England and Belgium, the firm was able not only to persevere, but to thrive.

Much of the credit for rescuing the company has been attributed to the colorful and confident Camille. At social events her entry was always awaited with great expectation: Roederer for everyone on the house.

It wasn't until 1975 that she retired, whereupon her grandson Jean-Claude Rouzaud took the wheel. Under Jean-Claude's tenure the firm acquired land and started a champagne house in California's Anderson Valley.

The company still owns vineyards in the Montagne de Reims (in the Parc naturel régional de la Montagne de Reims), the Marne Valley and the Côte des Blancs, the premier areas for growing pinot noir, pinot meunier and chardonnay grapes, the three types combined to make most champagne blends. Camille's great-grandson took over the business in 2006. The firm continues to be among the few of the large champagne houses that continue to be family owned, and that still carry on the tradition of aging champagnes in wooden casks – some for as long as six years on the lees.

The process of champagne making

Champagne crafting

The science of champagne making adds several levels of complexity to wine production, particularly with regard to harvesting, bottling and fermentation. Champagne grapes – namely pinot noir, pinot meunier but especially chardonnay – are cut by hand and gathered earlier to gain fresher, crisper tastes. Bottles must be specially designed and crafted to withstand the pressures of carbonation. Fermentation happens twice – once in vats, casks or barrels, and then again in the bottles.

Basically the steps of champagne making include the following: viticulture (the planting, tending and pruning of vineyards), harvesting, pressing, 1st fermentation, blending, bottling, 2nd fermentation, ridding (*remuage*), corking, aging, labelling, promoting, shipping (while maintaining acceptable temperatures and care of handling during long-distance journeys to an international clientele).

Champagne remains the sole quality French wine that does not display its A.O.C. or *Appellation d'Origine Controllée* on the label. By virtue of the name »champagne« itself, however, the wine has been subjected to rigorous oversight and control, including the degree of pressing and the time on the lees (stems, seeds and skins).

At the time, and largely true on a continuing basis, the actual grape growers stay close to the land as far as their activities of planting, tending, harvesting and crushing. From that point small champagne houses carry out their own fermentations, blending, bottling, riddling, corking, labelling, distribution, shipping, marketing, and selling, and in the end count among the small number of complete operations that yield a limited supply of highly-coveted bottles. As has been true probably since its inception – a variety of methods can lead to the end result of »champagne«, namely the blended alcoholic sparkling beverage made from a combination – or single one – of pinot noir, chardonnay and pinot meunier grapes that have been grown within the region of Champagne and made according to the set requirements mandated by the French appellation regulations.

Champagne is bottled in ten different sizes, but only the half-bottle, bottle, and magnum are always released in the bottles in which they were fermented the second time. The Jeroboam and larger sizes are transferred under pressure (transvasage) from the standard 75-centilitre/25.4-fluid-ounce bottles, as are quarter-bottles. Outsize bottles include the Rehoboam, equivalent to 6 bottles (4.5 litres); Methusalah, 8 bottles (6 litres); Salmanazar, 12 bottles (9 litres); Balthazar, 16 bottles (12 litres); Nebuhanezzar, 20 bottles (15 litres).

In addition to the vineyard-to-bottle model, a considerable number of other alternative production approaches exist for champagne production. Cooperatives of vineyards can grow grapes for sale to brokers that then perform the actual blending, fermentation and bottling processes, for example. Or, at the other end of the equation, there are behemoths like Moët. Founded in 1743 by Claude Moët, in the 19th century the firm traded on the close friendship of Claude's grandson Jean-Rémy Moët and Napoléon to catapult the Moët champagne house into celebrity status. Now, with subsidiaries Mercier, Ruinart, Veuve Clicquot and Pommery, the company of Louis Vuitton Möet Hennessy dominates the champagne export business, but also markets as luxury other products as diverse as perfume, leather, watches and jewelry.

Like other drinks that have been designated in association with a particular area, only champagne from the Champagne region can be called »champagne«, much in the same way that »Scotch whisky« must come from Scotland and be produced according to a certain formula or the way that »bourbon« is controlled.

The imagery, style and flair of Art Nouveau

La Belle Epoque signifies the time between the 1890s until the beginning of World War I in 1914. This prosperous period of calm gave rise to a style that elevated concepts of theater, romance and beauty. Champagne implicitly enhanced the enjoyment of all three.

A breakthrough in lithographic color print making inspired many early 20th century artists to embrace posters as their medium of choice. One of the foremost designers in this area, Jules Chéret (1836–1932), rose from modest circumstances to become a major influence in the art world with his depictions of vivacious free-spirited women. His work burst with energy, color and fun. »Cherettes« quickly became collector's items.

In the early 1900s the art of labeling and posters came to the fore, presenting champagne as integral to celebration for all, aristocratic or not. Whereas wines from the Burgundy and Bordeaux regions had adopted a more masculine tone to their promotions, champagne showed elegant, alluring women. Within the champagne houses, special sections were devoted to design studios and print shops.

One of the artists who left an indelible mark on champagne's imagery left his native Prague and came to Paris in 1887. His style, originally known as Mucha style, later became known as Art Nouveau. The 1900 Paris Universal Exhibition spread his work worldwide, carrying his distinctive illustrations into the Arts and Crafts sectors across the globe.

Alphonse Maria Mucha (1869–1939) used a pastel palette to portray comely young women in in flowing robes with a soft Neoclassical look, usually surrounded by intertwining flowers. This combination of figures with a floral border vaguely evokes Gothic *mille-fleurs* tapestry where figures are superimposed on a overall floral pattern. Mucha's muted earthier versions became a hallmark of the era, particularly his designs for Ruinart and Möet & Chandon.

Mucha came to the United States and earned money to support his efforts toward Slavic nationalism. On his return to Prague he fashioned new interiors for the theater of fine arts and painted a mural in the city hall. Once Czechoslovakia won its independence after World War I, he designed new postage stamps, bank notes and other trappings of the new nation.

Another leading light in the Art Nouveau/Art Déco periods, Italian artist Leonetto Cappiello (1875–1942), sparked in the early 20th century. His vivid images used bigger-than-life allegory. An exuberant young woman, with skirts swirling and bodice unwrapping, holds high a gigantic glass with champagne, fizzing and cascading over the sides. Its explosive effervescence appears to be a chemical reaction.

The land

The region of Champagne-Ardenne

The term »Champagne« has been used to refer to a variety of different places and configurations throughout history. The Champagne-Ardenne region as it now is defined includes the Ardennes, Marne, Aube and Haute-Marne with *chef-lieux* or *département* seats at Charleville-Mezières, Chalons-en-Champagne, Troyes and Chaumont. The region is bounded by Belgium to the north, Lorraine to the east, Franche-Comté to the southeast, Bourgogne to the south, Ile de France to the west and Picardie to the northwest.

Ardennes, a word of Dutch derivation, refers to heavily wooded hills and ridges that form a part of the Givetian Ardennes mountain range that lies mainly in Belgium and Luxembourg, but extends into France. Both the Ardennes département and the Champagne-Ardenne region take their name from the mountains. The Wallonian section of Belgium uses »Ardenne« in the singular, but in France »Ardennes«, plural, prevails.

Five viticultural districts comprise Champagne-Ardenne: the Montagne de Reims, Vallée de la Marne, Côte des Blancs, Côte de Sézanne and the Aube. According to appellation control laws, three types of grapes may be used in the production of champagne, singly or in combination. Pinot noir grows mainly in the Montagne de Reims in northern Champagne and in the Aube. Chardonnay comes almost exclusively from the Côte des Blancs that runs south of that. Pinot meunier comes primarily from the Aube region in Champagne's southernmost area and the Vallée de la Marne southeast of Reims. Reims and Epernay serve as the region's primary commercial centers.

The landscape: terroir and chalky cliffs

Champagne from the Champagne region contains one certain unique characteristic inextricably bond to the region itself – one that nature bestowed on

4. Herman Darewski, *Push and Go! Waltz*, 1911.
5. Émile Berchmans, *Champagne l'Étincelle*, 1922.

the region millions of years ago, one into which that Romans burrowed for hundreds of miles and one that now acts as one essential ingredient for the superbly dry, elegant taste. Champagne starts and finishes with chalk.

As remnants from an inland sea that covered the Parisian basin some 70 million years ago, chalk deposits in Champagne differ by their concentration of lime and calcite due to high fossil content. This special mix of crumbly clay, limestone and shell fragments make the right combination for keeping the temperature constant, for retaining the right degree of moisture, and maintaining the ground loose enough for roots to penetrate.

Beyond the large swath of chalk that stretches from England's white Dover cliffs all the way to Eastern Europe, conditions within the Champagne region itself vary considerably. Greater or lesser concentrations of shells, lime, and clay exist within the chalk deposits in the hills and valleys of the Marne and Seine, depending on how the chalk originated at the time the Parisian basin lay underwater. Such inconsistencies have given rise to the notion of *terroir*, the importance of specific location to the quality of grapes that reasonably may be expected to be produced there.

For the most part, grand cru villages sit on belemnite chalk, characterized by cylinder-shaped shells and believed to be superior because it gives grapes higher levels of acidity and aids photosynthesis. Topsoils in Champagne generally tend to be a thin layer over the chalk and consist of a mixture the usually includes sand, clay, brown coal and shells.

Originally twelve villages were designated as »grand cru« and given the rating of 100%. The number has been expanded to these 17: Ambonnay, Avize, Aÿ, Beaumont-sur-Vesle, Bouzy, le Mesnil-sur-Oger, Oger, Oiry, Puisieulx, Sillery, Tours-sur-Marne, Verzenay, Verzy. The rating system is known as *échelle des crus*, or »ladder of growth«. Premier cru ranks between 90 and 99%.

The system developed in response to the disparity of advantage between the champagne houses – who could buy grapes from increasingly distant vineyards – and the growers who sought more stability in their markets. The phylloxera infestation exacerbated the growers' dilemma and forced the issue to be resolved. Today the imbalance has been addressed further by the large number of grower cooperatives that press the grapes from their villages together and produce either »grand cru« or »premier cru« champagnes under numerous different labels.

Chalk is the reason that the stems are kept with the juice after the press. Tastes from the chalky ground come up through the roots and trunks to the stems of the vine; full clusters of grapes are cut from the vines so that the taste from the stems can be transmitted to the juice, or »must«. A white porous form of limestone, chalk allows the right amount of moisture to be held for the roots, but also provides for good drainage.

Chalk also plays a key role in the subsequent stages of champagne production; it gives the suitable conditions for the long-term aging period necessary for premium champagnes. Particularly in Reims where Louise Pommery put the old Roman tunnels to good use for her longer-aging brut champagnes, miles of underground spaces continue to be maintained for the storage and aging required by today's techniques.

The cultural commerce centers of Reims and Epernay

While once the textile trade and champagne fair commerce centered on the town of Troyes, the champagne trade revolves around Reims and Epernay. Historically Troyes and Reims suffered devastation time after time throughout their recorded histories, from the Romans onward. Troyes, the premier city during the prime eras of the Champagne fairs and long celebrated for its textiles, now stands as a museum to its illustrious past. At every corner its beautiful half-timbered buildings and narrow path-like streets evoke a long-gone grandeur. Reims, now more than three times the size of Troyes, flourishes as a center of the champagne trade, serving as the home to many of the major houses.

As part of a ten-year plan Reims has instituted a new tram system, rerouted traffic patterns to enhance its monuments, most notably the Roman Porte de Mars, and is implementing a pedestrian street – bustling with restaurants and farmers markets – that already stretches several blocks and ultimately is slated to reach all the way to the river.

The parks

Two regional parks created in the 1970's keep Champagne green. A pillar of the region's strength comes from the beauty of its landscape and the devotion to its preservation.

Le Parc naturel régional de la Montagne de Reims

Revolving around a long flat tableland known as »le plateau de la Montagne de Reims«, the rest of the park surrounding it is divided into three other sections. La côte de l'Ile-de-France stretches along its northern boundary, bending up north to the west and down south to the east, while clinging to the downward slopes of the plateau. Le tardenois de la Vallée de l'Ardre sits directly west and to the north, while the Vallée de la Marne forms the park's southernmost border as it follows the river.

Beginning in 1970 the mayors of three communes in Champagne conceptualized creation of a park as a way to protect against deforestation and to give safeguard a gateway to the region's interior. Four stated objectives continue to be research and preservation relating to the biological integrity of the area; to enact regulations to prevent extinguishing of agricultural vitality, including the issuance of building and demolition permits, with an eye to preserving historic sites; to advance environmental education; to encourage a local economy and activities that promote high ecological standards, including the safeguarding of biological diversity, such as the famous *faux de verzy* trees.

Now that mountain reigns as the place for premier, pinot noir grapes. To compensate for the

cooler climes and to gain intensity of taste, the vines are carefully trimmed back to encourage concentration of energy in the grape clusters and individual berries. The lands are also protected from over-development and imprudent use by strictures of the regional park that came into being in 1976. It was the second park to be created in the heart of Champagne country, after Parc naturel régional de la Forêt d'Orient was formed to the east of Troyes in 1970.

Le Parc naturel régional de la Forêt d'Orient

Groves and wetlands, with small farms and villages tucked inbetween; this is the feel of the newly reconfigured park to the south of the Champagne region. A certain sense of newness still may hang in the air because of the relative recent creation of the park itself. Despite their youthful age, though, the lakes brought to the area by the diversion of the Aube River have quickly gained popularity as recreational and resort destinations.

In the mid 1960s the artificial lakes of Lac d'Orient, Lac du Temple and Lac Amance were formed as flood control measures. The Aube River, which joins the Seine just north of Troyes, was partially diverted just to the south of the small town of Juvanzé in order to regulate the flow of the Seine River that begins near Dijon and continues through Troyes and Paris on its path to Le Havre and the English Channel. As early as 853 and repeatedly in the 16th century there is evidence of the Seine having flooded; both Troyes and Paris in particular have been plagued by inundations from the Seine.

The Fôret d'Orient and the Lac du Temple take their names from the 11th century Knights Templar who came from this area originally and used to hunt in the woods here. Previously known as the Fôret du Temple, the Knights took their name originally during the crusades because of their association with an area that had reputedly been Solomon's temple in Jerusalem at an earlier time. The Middle East was commonly referred to as the Orient in the Middle Ages.

The limitation on growth of companies hungry to expand operations has led to a side benefit experienced on a global basis. As one dramatic example, by 1973 Moët & Chandon was quietly acquiring lands in the central and southern Napa Valley that it slated for vineyards, indubitably in anticipation of the coming delimitation the 1976 park creation would bring. In California now numerous French companies produce sparkling wine – Taittinger, Mumm, Roederer included – but also places like New Zealand, Australia, Chile, South Africa have benefited from champagne companies' quest for more space. (Meanwhile Moët has agglomerated into a multi-dimensional corporation of luxury goods Moët Hennessy Louis Vuitton.)

Champagne continues to benefit from its prime position at a continental crossroads. Hundreds of years after Rome had been overthrown in the 5th century, the same roads that had once been used to connect far-flung parts of its empire continued to bring wayfarers to the Champagne fairs in the Middle Ages. Friesian, Saxon, Thuringian, Bavarian and Alamanni tribes are thought to have occupied the areas that bounded the Frankish kingdom to the east. During the second half of the 6th century the northern Champagne region was part of a frontier province that neighbored these Germanic tribes along the Rhine River. (The southern part area belonged to the interior province of Burgundians with Lyon as its center.) For such tribes living in proximity to each other, trading occurred naturally and regularly.

Even as boundaries shifted with the rise and fall of empires, day-to-day mercantile activities among neighbors probably endured more reliably than political ones. As the Champagne fairs had routinely drawn Europeans to the Champagne region, the business of wine – and later champagne – attracted broad regional interest and support. From Veuve Clicquot's business partner to the well-respected Krug Champagne house, the development of champagne has drawn regional participation that ignores political and other potential dividing lines.

In nascent stages export also played an early important role, especially with England and Russia, and later with the United States. While these countries continue to provide a steady demand, others like Brazil have joined the ranks as top champagne consumers. As soon as bottles were adequately sealed, cases of champagne made their way to all points of the globe, with an ever-expanding market penetration.

Laws and regulations that keep the Champagne region agricultural seem to have further elevated recognition and demand. An estimated 2500 other concerns actively conduct champagne-related affairs in the Champagne-Ardenne.

References

Medieval history

Biget, Jean-Louis, and Boucheron, Patrick, *L'Histoire par les sources. La France médiévale. Tome I: VIe –XII siècle,* Hachette, Paris, 1998.

Czmara, Jean-Claude, *Sur les Traces des Templiers, Circuit des Possessions Templières dans l'Aube*, Association Hugues de Payns, DRAC Campagne-Ardenne.

Demurger, Alain, *Les Templiers,* Editions Jean-Paul Gisserot, Luçon, 2007.

Joinville & Villehardouin, *Chronicles of the Crusades*, Penguin Books, London, 1963.

Jotischky, Andrew, and Caroline Hull, *Historical Atlas of the Medieval World*, Penguin, London, 2005.

Naert, Dominique, *Histories, légendes et mystères de Troyes,* Les Editions de la Maison du Boulanger, Troyes, 1999.

Polo de Beaulieu, Marie-Anne, *La France au Moyen Age: De l'An mil à la Pest Noire (1348)*, Les Belles Lettres, Paris, 2004.

Tierney, Brian, *The Middle Ages, Volume I: Sources of Medieval History*, McGraw-Hill College, New York, 1999.

Wine and champagne

Bird, David, *Understanding Wine Technology: The Science of Wine Explained*, DBQA, Newark, 2005.

De la Chaize, Angélique, and Éric Glatre, *Champagne: Pleasure shared*, Editions Hoëbeke, Paris, 2000.

Edwards, Jeremy, and Sheilagh Ogilvie, *What Lessons for Economic Development Can We Draw from the Champagne Fairs?* (April 29, 2011). CESifo Working Paper Series, No. 3438. Available at SSRN: http://ssrn.com/abstract=1837310.

Juhlin, Richard, *Champagne Guide*, Richard Juhlin Publishing, Stockholm, 2008.

Kladstrup, Don, and Petie, *Champagne: How the World's Most Glamorous Wine Triumphed Over War and Hard Times*, HarperCollins Publishers, New York, 2005.

Liger-Belair, Gérard, *Uncorked: The Science of Champagne*, Princeton University Press, New Jersey, 2004.

Mazzeo, Tilar J., *The Widow Clicquot: The Story of a Champagne Empire and the Woman who Ruled it*, HarperCollins Publishers, New York, 2008.

Pellechia, Thomas, *Wine: The 8,000-Year-Old Story of the Wine Trade*, Thunder's Mouth Press, New York, 2006.

Pellus, Daniel, *Femmes Célèbres de Champagne*, Martelle Editions, Bar-le-Duc, 1998.

Phillips, Rod, *A Short History of Wine*, HarperCollins Publishers, New York, 2000.

Ray, Cyril, *Bollinger: Tradition of a Champagne Family*, Heinemann, London, 1994.

Seward, Desmond, *Monks and Wine*, Mitchell Beazley Publishers Ltd., London, 1979.

Simon, André L., *The History of Champagne*, Octopus Books Ltd., London, 1971.

Stevenson, Tom, *Champagne*, Sotheby's Publications, London, 1988.

Sutcliffe, Serena, *Champagne*: *The History and Character of the World's Most Celebrated Wine*, Simon and Schuster, New York, 1988.

Taber, George M., *Judgment of Paris*: *California vs. France and the Historic 1976 Paris Tasting that Revolutionized Wine,* Scribner, New York, 2005.

Art Nouveau

Appelbaum, Stanley, *The Complete »Masters of the Poster«,* Dover Publications, New York, 1990.

Escritt, Stephen, *l'Art nouveau*, Phaidon, Paris, 2002.

Fahr-Becker, Gabriele, *Art Nouveau*, Ullmann/Tandem Verlag, English edition, Bonn, 2007.

Gallo, Max, *The Poster in History*, Norton, New York, 1972.

Parks

Delaforce, Patrick, *The Nature Parks of France,* The Windrush Press, Gloucestershire, England, 1995.

Le Guide Vert, Champagne Ardenne, Michelin, Paris, 2011.

Parc naturel régional de la Forêt d'Orient, Office de Tourisme, 2010–11.

Parc naturel régional de la Montagne de Reims. Découverte des Parcs de France, Itinéraires Touristiques, Institut Geographique National, 2007.

1, 2. Roman-era tunnels under the former residence of Barbe-Nicole Ponsardin in Reims.

3, 4. Roman-era vaulting under the Place du Forum, Reims.

pp. 26/27
5. Porte de Mars, Reims.

6. Gallo-Roman site in Andilly.
7. Gallo-Roman ruins in Andilly.

8. Blois. View across the Loire River.
9. Medieval tower in Blois.

10. 19th-century reconstruction of medieval Blois castle.
11. 19th-century reconstruction of medieval Blois castle. Interior.

12, 13. Abbaye de St. Loup, Troyes. Walkways.

14. Medieval streetscape in Troyes.
15. Maison d'Allemand, Troyes.

pp. 38/39
16. Maison d'Outils, Troyes.

17. Aube River near the former Champagne fair site in Bar-sur-Aube.
18. Aube River in Bar-sur-Aube.

19, 20. Tower and ramparts in Provins.

pp. 44/45
21. Half-timbered house dating to the Middle Ages in Provins.

22, 23. Souterrains in Provins.

24. Château du Marché in the Petit Jard, Châlons-en-Champagne.
25. Former site of champagne fairs next to the abbey in Lagny-sur-Marne.

26. Gardens at the former residence of Barbe-Nicole Ponsardin Clicquot on Rue Cérès, Reims.
27. Former residence of Barbe-Nicole Clicquot on Place du Forum, Reims. Now Musée Le Vergeur.

28. Former Pommery residence in Chigny-les-Roses.
29. Pommery champagne cellars in Reims.

30. Staircase to Pommery champagne cellars in Reims.
31. Parc de Champagne, Reims, gift of Jeanne Pommery.

32. View of the Parc naturel régional de la Montagne de Reims from Chigny-les-Roses.
33. Square in Chigny-les-Roses, honoring Jeanne Pommery.

pp. 58/59
34. View of the Parc naturel régional de la Montagne de Reims from Chigny-les-Roses.

35. Newer model wine press in Mesnil-sur-Oger, Côte des Blancs.
36. Older model wine press in Mesnil-sur-Oger.

37. Delamotte champagne cellars in Mesnil-sur-Oger, Côte des Blancs.
38. Martel champagne cellars in Reims.

pp. 64, 65
39. Gate to the Pommery champagne vineyards in Reims.
40. Gate to the Taittinger champagne cellars in Pierry.

pp. 66, 67
41, 42. Taittinger champagne cellars from the Gallo-Roman era in Reims.

43. Riddling racks in the Moët & Chandon champagne cellars in Epernay.
44. Riddling racks in the Pommery champagne cellars in Reims.

pp. 70/71
45. Chalk walls in the Taittinger champagne cellars in Reims.

46–48. Vineyards near Aÿ in the Parc naturel régional de la Montagne de Reims.

49. Vineyards in the Parc naturel régional de la Montagne de Reims.
50. Vineyards near Bouzy in the Parc naturel régional de la Montagne de Reims.

51. Winery in Bouzy, Parc naturel régional de la Montagne de Reims.
52. Lodging in Bouzy.

pp. 78/79
53. City hall in Bergères-Les-Vertus, Côte des Blancs.

54. Square in Sézanne, Côte de Sezanne.
55. Le Mail des Cordeliers, Sézanne.

pp. 82/83
56. City hall in Sézanne.

pp. 84/85
57. Marne River in the Parc naturel régional de la Montagne de Reims.

58. Marne River in Cumières.
59. Bridge over the Marne River in Cumières.

60. Aube River near St. Nabord.
61. Aube River just before the flood-control diversion, north of Jessains.

62, 63. Vineyards near Celles-sur-Ource, Aube.
64. Fields near Celles-sur-Ource.

pp. 92/93
65. Chalk cliffs in the Parc naturel régional de la Montagne de Reims.

66, 67. Chalk cliffs near Tours-sur-Marne.

68. Fountain on Place Drouet d'Erlon, Reims.
69. Cathédrale Notre-Dame de Reims.

70. Bibliothèque Carnegie, Reims. Art deco light fixture.
71. Bibliothèque Carnegie, Reims. Reading room.

72. Jardin Henri Deneux, Reims.
73. Hotel des Crayères, Reims.

74. Market on Place Drouet d'Erlon, Reims.
75. Villa Demoiselle, Reims.
76. Half-timbered house at Place du Forum, Reims.

77. Vertical garden in Reims.
78. Art-deco passage in Reims.

79. Square Saint-Nicaire, Reims.
80. Municipal park in Reims.

81. Epernay. View from Tour de Castellane.
82. Epernay with Marne River.

83, 84. Municipal park in Epernay.
85. Epernay with Marne River.

86. Hautvillers, Parc naturel régional de la Montagne de Reims, with Marne River.
87. Vineyards near Hautvillers.

88. Faux de Verzy, Forêt Domaniale de Verzy.
89. Forêt Domaniale de Verzy. Walking path.

90. Canal rejoining Aube River, Parc naturel régional de la Forêt d'Orient.
91. Spillway sculpture by Klaus Rinke in the Parc naturel régional de la Forêt d'Orient.

92. Environmental education building in the Parc naturel régional de la Forêt d'Orient.
93. Roofed bird-watching platform in the Parc naturel régional de la Forêt d'Orient.

94. Half-timbered house in Brienne, Parc naturel régional de la Forêt d'Orient.
95. Covered market in Brienne.

96. Building in Géraudot, Parc naturel régional de la Forêt d'Orient.
97. Columbier in Dienville, Parc naturel régional de la Forêt d'Orient.
98. Columbier in Dienville. Dome.

99. Champigny-sur-Aube.
100. Windmill in the Parc naturel régional de la Forêt d'Orient.

pp. 126/127
101. Lac d'Orient in the Parc naturel régional de la Forêt d'Orient.